How to Buy an RV Without Getting Ripped Off

JD Gallant

SECOND EDITION

D0063505

Quilcene, Washington

How to Buy an RV Without Getting Ripped Off

© 1997 JD Gallant

Quill Publishing
Box 490 • Quilcene, WA 98376

Gallant, JD
　　　How to Buy an RV Without Getting Ripped Off
　　　ISBN 1-884046-64-9 $12.95   1997
　　　1. Buying an RV--Purchasing. 2. Recreational
　　　Vehicles--Purchasing
I. Gallant, JD   II. Title:
　　　How to Buy an RV Without Getting Ripped Off

The Library of Congress has previously catalogued another edition as follows:
　　　　　Catalog Card Number: 93-85201

NOTICE

The information in this book is designed to guide — not to direct. It is strictly opinion based on personal experiences and research. It is the author's intention to correct any inaccuracies by periodically providing updates, new editions, and notices of any error. The author or publisher assumes no responsibilities for inconveniences or damages resulting from the use of this material. All users are encouraged to use this book in the manner for which it is intended.

Printed in the United States of America

About the Author

JD Gallant has been an RV enthusiast and RV trekker for over 30 years. Besides loving the fun and adventures of RVing, he has actively worked as a technical writer, teacher, RV salesperson, and advisor for many years. Through his books, seminars, and workshops he has guided thousands of RVers on the right path to searching, buying, and enjoying their motor homes, travel trailers, and campers.

JD is contributing editor to *the RVLookout* and president of RV Consumer Group, a nonprofit organization.

Special Fund Raising Edition

Quill Publishing dedicates the net proceeds of this book to the building of RV Consumer Group's training and research centers.

Thank you for your support!

ACKNOWLEDGMENTS

To the staff and members of RV Consumer Group, I extend my thanks for your support and insights. I especially appreciate the assistance and team support of Roy Easton and Glenn Sharp.

Special thanks to my publisher, Connie Bernardo, who manages to keep everything flowing with an encouraging attitude and unwavering determination.

I must also thank the people of T/Maker Company for helping dress up the book with the use of ClickArt® Images, their copyrighted artistic works.

My gratitude to Ralph Nader and staff for pioneering so many consumer awareness programs. He has been my role model in my years of study and research.

This book is dedicated to the memory of my friend
Ed Lackman,
whom I greatly miss; and to
Margaret Gallant,
my sharp, quick-witted, and wonderful Mom who
lived a full life of 95 years.

Table of Contents

- ❖ How long should I plan ahead?
- ❖ Why choose type first?
- ❖ How does size really limit me?
- ❖ Let's face it, isn't the quality pretty much the same in all brands?
- ❖ What if the only floor plan I like is in a lower quality RV?
- ❖ Why is price last when everyone else puts it first?

- ❖ Should I ask these questions at first or spread them out?
- ❖ What about questions relating to tow vehicles?
- ❖ Should I ask about competitor's brands?
- ❖ Can you give me an example of what I can ask and what I should get for an answer?

- ❖ What should I say when I first walk into an RV dealership?
- ❖ What will an MSRP sheet really tell me?
- ❖ How do I compare one RV brand with another — especially if I decide to go used?
- ❖ How about buying from a private party?

- ❖ How do RV salespeople qualify a buyer?
- ❖ What is a trial close?
- ❖ What is a "turn"?
- ❖ When and how do I control the leaving?

Introduction

Don't let the title of this book fool you. Although the book is designed for RV (recreational vehicles) buyers, it should be used as a guide for all big-ticket purchases. Buying an RV requires the same techniques as buying a car, a truck, a boat, a mobile home, or real estate. The salespeople come from the same mold. The business owners have similar philosophies. You and your neighbor have buying habits that could probably be exchanged without notice. What you learn here, therefore, should save you hundreds of times the cost of this book.

The ten rules outlined in this book are easy to follow. I have students who have made unbelievable buys while getting what they need and want by following these ten rules. The book is meant to be compact; so if you have to slow down now and then to think about what's being said, consider it normal. Reference material is noted in the text and in the back of the book.

Following the ten rules of this book will pit you against the odds of throwing away $6,000 — the amount the average buyer throws away by buying wrong or paying too much. The rewards for accepting this adventure head-on will be great. You'll go farther and be happier. You'll be proud of yourself for buying right. You'll make friends by helping others. The adventure will never stop.

If I write a bit harshly about RV salespeople, please don't judge me too fast. I've been on many sales lots as a consumer and as a salesperson. Every day I hear horror stories of people who have lost most of their savings to the hot-shots. That I have a bias for the RV consumer is not in question. I freely admit it is so. After you've read the book completely and followed the rules, you can write to me and tell me if you think I'm off base.

The following is part of a commentary on **RV** discount houses that I wrote for *the RVLookout* — an **RV** consumer newsletter. These excerpts might help illuminate my viewpoint about RV salespeople.

---

saw one get caught in grand style. This young man got caught because the element of urgency was there. His dream was to take his young family on a cross-country trip before the progression of serious illness in one of the family members prevented this dream from happening. It was a now or never scenario. He got caught in the web. His statement was: *"I would never believe it could happen to me. With my vast experience in handling people, I was smoothly manipulated by an expert. I believed him when he said it was an unbelievable buy. He was trustable. He was smooth. I bit. I don't like what I bought, and I paid $15,000 too much. I just don't believe I did it."*

I saw another get caught in the web. This one was snared so quickly and tightly that I'm not sure he ever knew what happened. This "well-experienced" RVer left with a 350 C.I.D. (5.7L) Chevrolet engine pulling an 11,000 GVWR fifth wheel — and the 3/4 ton truck had a short bed! (Specification per GM is 8400 pounds maximum trailer weight.) When I saw the trailer leaving on a downhill slope, it couldn't even make a 70-degree turn from the lot without hitting the truck cab. Both truck and trailer were new. One of the two would have to be replaced at a big loss. I heard the statement from the salesperson on this one. *"Put in an RV cam,"* he said, *"and it'll work fine. I'll even deduct the cost from the trailer price."* The buyer wanted to believe. He was still believing when I last

Courtesy: *the RVLookout*

saw him.

I was appraising a 2 year-old fifth wheel when an older couple walked in to take another look at their purchase of just a few minutes before. *"We weren't ready to buy until fall,"* the small gray-haired lady said, *"but it's so pretty and the price is so good that we decided to buy today."* The couple paid about $15,000 and the book retail was closer to $10,000. When I finished the appraisal on their unit, the score was 3 on a scale of 1 to 10 — with 10 being the highest.

This couple didn't know about the quality of RVs because they had never owned one. They judged the RV from a narrow perspective, and they trusted the salesperson to take care of their needs. That the ceiling had major defects would have been impossible for them to know. They hadn't read *The Green Book—RVs Rated* or *The RV Rating Book* so they couldn't know this particular manufacturer doesn't do very well at putting RVs together.

Not everyone gets caught. One buyer confided that he caught the salesperson changing direction with each RV entered. *"He was smooth at it,"* he said. *"If I hadn't been on the ball, I would have been taken in. He was so good that I might have bought. I knew just enough to catch him."*

RVers need to know enough to stay out of the web. They need to know if the deal is fair. They need to buy right at a dealership that can service their needs. Part of the sales presentation should be about the dealership — its service, its history, its future — and the salesperson. RVers need to be happy about their purchase for more than six months.

There are those who believe that bursting the bubble will blow the dream. Not so! Bursting the bubble that all RVs are the same will make for happier RVing. Bursting the bubble that all RV salespeople can be trusted will help get RVers into the right RVs. Bursting the bubble that you get a better deal on price alone will help RV consumers make better buying decisions.

Bursting the bubble will help some — but not all. On a sunny day it's easy to get caught.

About Smoothy

Now, something about Smoothy, the main character in this book.

Smoothy is a composite of real salespeople. Smoothy exists. The statements quoted came from the mouths of real Smoothies. Don't expect Smoothy to be a man or a woman. Don't expect Smoothy to be young or old. Don't expect Smoothy to smile, to frown, to be friendly,  or unfriendly. Don't expect Smoothy to be talkative, to be smart, or to like you. Smoothy is only one thing: a practitioner of getting you into an RV at Smoothy's profit.

If you think you know who Smoothy is, you're wrong — unless, of course, you signed the papers then came off the high. You only know Smoothy after the fact. Like a doctor who does nothing for you but does a lot to you. Like a lawyer who holds out the hand after losing a case that couldn't be lost.

There is only one way to find and outsmart Smoothy: follow the ten rules in this book. Because you want to go RVing, I know you will accept the challenge. You've got to deal before you wheel.

Rule 1

Prepare to choose in the correct order!

The correct order for choosing an RV is as follows:
1) type, 2) size, 3) quality, 4) floor plan, and 5) price.
Most RVers make serious mistakes in more than one of these areas. The proof is in the number of almost-new RVs on the sales lots. Every RV traded before five years costs the owner thousands of dollars. Consider:

Buying wrong results in nonuse.
Buying wrong causes changes in travel plans.
Buying wrong results in frustration.
Buying wrong makes for a poor investment.
Buying wrong makes Smoothy richer —
                    and you poorer.

Although the investment in your RV is influenced by all five areas, size is the number one <u>reason</u> for change with type a close second. When it comes to changing, it seems that motor homes win first place. (It may be like Thanksgiving dinner — bigger eyes than stomach.)

When you look at an RV, your emotions will get in the way of your needs. It <u>will</u> happen. The anticipation of going over the next hill or into the wilderness will tend to cloud conservative buying habits. It happens to all of us. To make a good buy, logic must overpower emotion.

How long should I plan ahead?

If you don't have a time frame, it's almost impossible to have good direction. History has proven that RVers generally trade within five years with big losses. Societal changes have a big impact. The statement *"I plan on keeping it for twenty years,"* is rarely heard today because it sounds silly. Unfortunately, some RV manufacturers are taking advantage of this trend by building disposable RVs. This marketing technique compounds the problem of premature failures and extreme waste at a time when old RVs are plaguing the countryside.

You need to look five years into your personal future. Look at your desire to travel. Look at your enjoyment of primitive camping. Try to determine the kind of campgrounds where you'll be staying. To help determine where you're going, study the maps of North America — always include Canada and Mexico in your 5-year plan. If you plan on going easterly more than westerly, you may want a different size or type. If you plan on snowbirding or fulltiming, you'll definitely need to look seriously at quality, size, and floor plan.

If you ignore the 5-year plan, it'll be like buying a house without checking the foundation. You would never do that — would you?

Plan 5 years ahead!

Why choose type first?

Don't even begin to get serious until you decide on the type of RV you'll need for your RVing adventures. Salespeople will try to influence you, your friends will try to influence you, and your neighbors will tell you what they think. Most will add to the confusion. If you keep in mind that the type of RV you choose is the very first aspect of the buying decision, you'll be more apt to sift information when you and your spouse sit alone. You must consider type, size, quality, floor plan, and price to prepare for your 5-year plan, but always keep type ahead of the rest.

To choose type, as in choosing size, quality, floor plan, and price, you need to determine what you will be doing with the RV. Let's break it down into four uses: 1) vacationing, 2) RV trekking, 3) snowbirding, and 4) fulltiming. (If you need definitive explanations of these uses, refer to my book, *The Language of RVing*.)

The small motor home, for example, is an ideal vacation RV. You can get around easily, be ready to go in a very short time, and can accommodate almost any size family. With the right motor

Class A Motor Home

Class B
Motor Home

home you can pull a small boat or car with ease. The motor home shows its strengths when there's lots of traveling on a short term basis. It might work well for snowbirding in the longer sizes if travel is a priority. If living for four months without travel is a priority, I have found that motor homes do not work as well as travel trailers.

Class C Motor Home

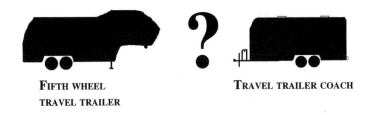

Fifth wheel
travel trailer

Travel trailer coach

Fifth wheel travel trailers tend to work best for RV trekking and other lifestyles requiring a live-aboard situation. Travel trailer coaches under 25 feet work well for vacationing at campgrounds while 30 feet and under work well for snowbirding. Since budget is an important factor in choosing type, you should study initial cost, mileage costs, and depreciation for each type. As an example, I find motor homes generally cost more on both initial expense and per mile basis than travel trailers.

Don't let anyone dissuade you from putting type ahead of size, quality, floor plan, and price. If the type is wrong, all else will be wrong.

How does size really limit me?

The trend during the eighties was to go big. Unfortunately, those who pushed that trend in the eighties are selling big in the nineties because they're geared for it. But things have changed. The traffic is much heavier, parking is becoming a serious problem, and the average camping site has shrunk by five feet. You can't fight size as being an important factor. Everybody's trying to, but it won't work. The manufacturers can put more glitter (and profit) into a 30-foot than a 25-foot motor home or travel trailer. Even though we know large motor homes are monsters on the highways, neophyte RVers are still buying them by the thousands. Long, wide-bodied motor homes and fifth wheels are being built by those manufacturers who care little about your 5-year plan. Their priority is to get you off the sales lot with new license plates. After that, it's your problem.

Too big is too big!

Watch out for wide-bodies. Watch out for big slides. Watch out for multiple slides. Watch out for large and cheap. These are realistic and simple cautions. As you fight emotion with logic, keep these cautions before you. Because you're probably used to a big house, you're apt to want the biggest RV you can handle. Size will be the number one appealing factor.

Let's face it, isn't the quality pretty much the same in all brands?

If manufacturers and salespeople could convince you of this, their lives would be easier. That all brands are not created equal can be easily proven on your own by following the simple guidelines you'll be studying in Rule 5. If you don't think you can do well at appraising, use *The RV Rating Book* as your guide.

Salespeople usually try to avoid questions of comparison. When you ask about brands, Smoothy will hem and haw. Watch his eyes when you get into the subject. From the basic knowledge you begin to accumulate, you'll be able to make a good judgement on whether his words are credible opinion or bull.

No RV is good enough. You might as well begin to believe it now because you're going to find out it's a fact of life.

It's not hard to check an RV on your own. All of my students learn to check two areas that set the pulse for quality: the galley and the roof. If you use *The RV Rating Book* as a gauge for safety and quality, don't waste your time on RVs rated below 70 — unless it's to satisfy curiosity. We'll get more into appraising later.

If you find your tastes developing above the strength of your checkbook, you may want to stay with the quality standard and switch to a good used RV. Keep in mind that 90% of RVers make big mistakes and want to trade within the 5-year time frame. Many of these RVs are as good as new. It takes a bit more work to find a good one with an acceptable floor plan for you, but the savings are often tremendous. If, however, you are planning on buying almost new, you still should make comparisons with new.

When all else fails, stay in budget!

What if the only floor plan I like is in a lower quality RV?

Floor plans are never perfect. You'll find the worse manufacturers can have some of the best floor plans because they ignore basic construction techniques required for efficient use and good handling. You will most assuredly find the cheapest RVs loaded with cabinets and wardrobes. These manufacturers won't tell you there's no way you can use them without throwing the vehicle out of balance or that the payload capacity is nowhere near enough to fill these storage areas with anything except pillows. Compromises will probably have to be made — especially in the areas of storage and capacity. Once you're on the road, you'll learn very fast that you can't take everything you own with you.

Study the floor plans. Be sure the brochures have details you can understand when you review them at home. Until you make up your mind on type, you'll have to compare

I really like this one, but I can't see a place where I can store that set of china my mother gave us.

There's always a compromise!

floor plans of travel trailer coaches, fifth wheels, and motor homes. You'll soon see there are obvious differences that limit floor plans in some types.

If you come across a Smoothy in the first stages of your investigation, you'll find yourself being encouraged to sit in the seat of a motor home. You'll think of yourself as an airplane pilot — having the thrill of pushing buttons and pulling levers as you control this vehicle while zooming down the highway towards great adventures. If Smoothy knows of a bonus on a trailer with particularly big windows, he'll draw pictures in your mind of the beautiful view you'll have as you sit on the rim of a great canyon or by the side of a wilderness lake. If he thinks he can get you excited over a runabout motor home, you'll find him pushing the practicality of good mileage and easy access to shopping center parking stalls. All of this needs to be pointed out, but the floor plan that seems practical on the sales lot might not work in real RVing.

Many neophytes get locked into a specific bed and bath configuration. Consider that twin beds are usually very efficient but can make spouses into strangers. Consider that front-to-rear walk-around beds are roomier but consume a lot of floor space. Consider that corner beds are space efficient but almost impossible to make up in the morning. Consider that small corner baths get old too soon, but that the larger rear baths eliminate tail-end views. The list is almost endless for compromises. It's something that has to be worked out carefully without pressure from others. The floor plan is the most personal decision of the five areas — and the major reason for premature trading.

Why is price last when everyone else puts it first?

The price is tied to your budget — and there's an RV for every budget. People get caught up in price because it's easy for dealers to advertise price and salespeople to sell on price. Price gets attention everywhere. Ninety percent of RVers look at price as number one. Once you focus on price, everything else takes a back seat. You need to replace price with budget. You need to counter the influences being pushed at you. The price will be forgotten as you see the cabinetry show premature wear. The price will be forgotten as you complain about the floor plan. The price will be forgotten as you realize you should have bought something else.

To accurately figure budget you need to stay focused on your crystal ball. Your budget should include <u>everything</u> for the next five years. It should be accurate within 10%. The list will be long and will take hours of work; but since Smoothy will almost always use price to get you to the closing desk, you'll need to keep focused on your budget. Price is not a major concern until you decide upon type, size, quality and floor plan — in that order.

If you sleep on the budget, Smoothy will get you!

Sure, a motor home will cost a lot if you don't use it. If you drive it, it'll pay for itself in five years. I put 30,000 miles on mine in two years.

Smoothy rarely knows anything about RVing that he hasn't learned on the sales lot. If Smoothy has traveled somewhat with an RV, all his learning has been haphazard at best.

The average mileage per year for motor homes before heavy depreciation takes place is about 4,000 miles. You'll pay dearly for each mile over that average. How much would you pay for a 4 year-old motor home that has 50,000 on the odometer? It surely wouldn't be anywhere near the value of the same motor home with 16,000. If you bring in a trade that has over average miles, watch Smoothy knock the dollars off the trade-in allowance.

Rule 2

Have 5 test questions ready

Prepare five questions from *The Language of RVing* to ask each RV salesperson you meet. You must, of course, know the answers. And, please, don't make them too easy. Any salesperson earning between $40,000 and $100,000 annually should be a professional and be able to answer almost any question you can throw at him or her. (Don't excuse women — they'll take your money just as fast as men.)

Don't be led and don't believe everything you hear. It's too early in the game to trust the players. You may need to fight the temptation to be nice. Think about the hard work it took to get the money you're planning to spend on this RV. Let's make it your decision all the way.

The questions you ask should pertain to your 5-year plan. If they are important, your sincerity will show to the salesperson. Some people take notes during the presentation — others after. You should do it according to your comfort zone. The notetaking is secondary — your feelings about the salesperson as a professional are paramount.

Don't let yourself feel guilty about putting on the pressure. The person standing before you earns at least $30 per hour — every hour! Don't expect less from an RV salesperson than you would from an RV technician.

If you don't have questions ready, you will never be in control of the buying process. This means that you will probably be one of those who keeps the $6,000 throwaway going. It all begins here. A few hours of preparation will save you thousands of dollars. Do it!

Should I ask these questions at first or spread them out?

You'll want to spread out your questions, but try to do it within the first 30 minutes. Since you're not yet an expert, don't give the salesperson a hint of where you're going. Your job at this time is solely to eliminate the salesperson who can't help you.

Begin by finding out how long the salesperson has been in the business. If he's a beginner, there's room for forgiveness. If he's been at it for years and still doesn't know anything, you should beware. All salespeople should know RV basics. Always ask if he owns an RV. Find out what type. Does he go RVing often? Probe! Probe!

Do not interrogate or badger. It's possible you'll have to work with a salesperson with whom you've had an active encounter. He may just a hard-working professional who doesn't know very much about RVs. Your neighborhood dealer may be the best to buy from, but you may have to make all the decisions without his help. Keep in mind that RV salespeople also have bad days. Customers who aren't friendly

Probe!
But watch out
for sharp teeth.

or courteous may set a mood that carries into your visit. Since you have control, you don't need to be nasty. Just do your thing by asking those five questions.

What about questions relating to tow vehicles?

Every RV salesperson should know about towing vehicles. I know one RV salesperson who still looks at the GVWR (Gross Vehicle Weight Rating) on the door pillar of the truck to tell his customers how heavy a trailer they can tow. The towing vehicle's GVWR, of course, does not tell you its trailer-towing capacity. There is absolutely no excuse for an RV salesperson not to have towing specs at his fingertips. Do not forgive any absence of this knowledge or the inability to provide the information. Life has been too easy for these so-called professionals. It's time for that to change.

Towing a motorized vehicle behind a motor home is more technically demanding than towing a trailer. If a mistake is made in choosing the right vehicle, the cost can be heavy. If the RV salesperson has information about dinghy towing in writing, give him an A$^+$. If the information is verbal, double check it.

Under no condition accept a *"Sure, it can pull this without a problem,"* or *"Sure, this can be pulled without a problem."* Watching a salesperson's lips move about towing specs is tantamount to asking for disaster. All the information you need is in the vehicle manufacturer's towing guide — whether a truck or a car.

Another concern is that the towing specifications by vehicle manufacturers are always liberal. Since there is big competition among pickup truck lines, manufacturers know they are going to lose sales if they can't say their trucks will

Don't worry, your truck will pull anything on this lot.

pull enough to satisfy the RVer. Since they're in the business to sell what they build, you can bet they'll give you the highest towing capacity they can justify. If an RV or truck salesperson says you can easily exceed the towing limit shown in the specification sheet, don't trust him with your money. Although some RVers do seem to get by exceeding these towing limits, the odds of premature wear and accidents are stacked against them. I've seen a half-ton truck pulling a 12,000 pound fifth wheel, and I don't ever want to be behind the wheel of such an overburdened vehicle. Towing guides are a must, and a maximum towing limit is absolutely a <u>maximum</u>.

Should I ask about competitor's brands?

If you really want to shake up a salesperson, ask him to compare his RVs to a competitor's brands. Most salespeople hate talking about the competition. They'll say they don't like knocking the other guy. You come back with, *"Don't knock it, just tell me the facts."* Wait for the response. Smoothy will usually dump you fast, but a good salesperson will hang in there.

To know about the competition is difficult for the RV salesperson who already has a hard time understanding about his own brands. He may have to take a day off to visit an RV show or another dealership. Unless he's forced into it, he'll never do it.

Finding out what the competition has to offer can be very scary to a salesperson.

If the salesperson tries to give a comparison presentation but can't seem to get it together, put the competitor's brochure next to his brochure on the RV's table. Compare construction features — especially roof, frame, and suspension. This is also a good chance to compare optional equipment. Make the salesperson work with you on the differences. Don't forget to make notes on the brochures. If you do this with every dealer you visit, you'll have a wealth of information at your fingertips.

Can you give me an example of what I can ask and what I should get for an answer?

Sure. Here are five simple questions and expected responses (ER). Keep in mind, however, that most of the answers should be quite extensive. Use *The Language of RVing* as a basis for your questions.

Q. How much does it weigh?

ER: The salesperson should show you the GVWR on the RV or in the brochure. If he throws out a figure without looking at the brochure or spec tag on the RV, you can almost bet he's guessing. If he goes for the gross dry weight or gross wet weight, push the issue. Ask for the maximum weight you'll be towing. Stand your ground. Don't settle for figures rolling off the tongue. If this information is not accurately given, put a 1 on this salesperson's business card.

Q. What size tow vehicle do I need?

ER: The answer to this one should be given to you carefully and with some thoughtfulness. The salesperson should find your needs before he makes a recommendation. He should pull out a towing guide and explain how it works in conjunction with the trailer specifications. This is, of course, a good time for him to take you to his office and attempt a trial close. Give him credit for trying — after all, that's his job.

Q. How is it insulated?

ER: With this question you should get more than a brochure response. If the salesperson is a professional, a question like this will give him a chance to show his stuff. He should get into R values and types of insulation. He should talk about the differences between aluminum and fiberglass as insulators. He should talk about the roof material and structure, and explain the overall R-value. (See 'R value' in *The Language of RVing*.)

Q. Do I need storm windows?

ER: When you ask this question, you'll get more opinions

than good answers. To answer this question correctly, the salesperson should ask you some very pertinent questions before he goes overboard with the technical stuff. After all, you may simply want to know if you need storm windows. He should talk about use, window size, condensation, and the overall insulation factor.

Q. How does this brand rate against a _____ ?
ER: Expect specifics on construction and interior quality. He should always use the real model for his argument. If he asks you where you saw the brand, it's okay to tell him. If he asks you about the price, <u>don't</u> tell him. The question should not allow him to go on a fishing expedition. You simply want accurate answers so you can make an intelligent buying decision. Tell him that if he wants your business he'll have to earn it — the old fashioned way.

Always take a flashlight, a notepad, and 5 questions.

Put in an RV cam and it'll work fine. I'll even deduct the cost from the trailer price.

I could hardly believe this one myself. I heard it with my own ears. The truck was rated to pull just under 3000 pounds less than the GVWR of the fifth wheel travel trailer. To make matters worse, the truck was a short bed and couldn't make a legal turn without the front of the fifth wheel hitting the cab. In this case, Smoothy knew exactly what he was doing.

Rule 3

Visit at least 5 dealerships

During your initial visits to the dealerships, you should make decisions on type, size, and quality. You'll need at least five dealers for this input. You'll need to collect retail prices and trade allowances if you have a trade. Write the retail price and the trade allowance in the brochure for future study. And, of course, you'll collect copies of MSRP sheets which you'll fasten to the appropriate brochures.

Don't be led by the nose. Demand facts. No facts, no talky. You must learn to control the buying decision from the very beginning. Be friendly, be firm.

Always keep in mind that your initial visits are to collect information. Expect a Smoothy to drop you fast if he senses you are on a research mission. Good salespeople, however, will take your name, address, and telephone number and offer to help you get the information you need.

Beware of dealerships that lock all RVs. Reasons for this policy are generally not valid. At the very least, expect some display models to be open. A closed lot usually indicates high pressure (and high profit) selling techniques. Keeping all RVs locked has been advocated by some sales-motivation experts as a device for controlled qualifying and presentations. Closed RVs have merits, but those merits do not generally benefit the consumer.

Visit the dealership's service area even if you do it on your own. Stand back and observe the technicians at work. Try to get a sense of proficiency. Give the service department at least five minutes of your time.

Try to eavesdrop on the salespeople. You'll be surprised at what you hear. Listening to RV salespeople talk with prospects will give you an idea of what you'll be facing.

It's fun if you do it right.

What should I say when I first walk into an RV dealership?

Your first approach is very important. I recommend calling the dealership first and talking to more than one salesperson. Ask pertinent questions about the dealership and its brands. Stay away from the technical stuff on the phone. If you feel comfortable with a particular salesperson, you may want to make an appointment. Keep in mind, however, that Smoothies are very good on the phone. Their objective is to get you to their desk. They know that most incoming telephone calls are gold-lined.

If a salesperson knows how to use the phone for prospecting, he'll get your name and number almost immediately. He'll find a reason for calling you

Hi! I'm Sue and I'm looking for an RV, but I don't know what kind I want or how much I should be paying. I am going to buy in about two months. I need a lot of questions answered because I read this book that said...

back. Expect aggressiveness. It's a sign of sales professionalism. Expect him to pump you for the 'urgency' factor. If you get an obvious nitwit or a Smoothy, don't give any information. If the reception is good after you tell him or her about your basic needs, you may want to find out the days and hours that the salesperson is working.

Whether you talk on the phone or in person, keep the impression going that you are a serious buyer. Never say, *"I'm just shopping,"* or *"I'm going to buy when I find the right RV."* Both of these statements do the wrong things. If you say "shopping", you either turn the salesperson off or get him into a fast

Hello Sue, this is Bill at First Place RV. I wanted to let you know the RV you liked so much was put on special this month. If you can come in today, I think I can arrange...

qualifying mode. If you say "buying", you are pushing a button for the sale today. Those in the business know that 'hot' buyers are itchy to hit the road. They also know that if these hot-to-trot prospects leave the lot, they'll probably never be seen again because they'll get caught at the competition. RVers who mention buying will be given fast tours, hit hard with trial closes, and get turned before they leave the lot. The pressure will be heavy. Be serious about buying, but try, *"I'm going to buy an RV in the near future."* This honest approach might get you that professional salesperson who will be willing to work with you.

What will an MSRP sheet really tell me?

A genuine MSRP (Manufacturer's Suggested Retail Price) sheet and a good brochure will tell you almost everything available in print about a particular model. You need both if you want to make a good purchase. Be sure you include a copy of the MSRP sheet in the brochure of any brand you may consider.

Study the drawing below. Notice the standard equipment column on the left. The same equipment will be listed in the

---

MANUFACTURER'S SUGGESTED RETAIL PRICE

DEALER	MANUFACTURING PLANT	INVOICE #

ADDRESS	BRAND MODEL COLOR	YEAR

VEHICLE SERIAL NUMBER	DATE OF MANUFACTURE

THE FOLLOWING ITEMS ARE STANDARD ON THIS MODEL AT NO EXTRA CHARGE	MANUFACTURER'S SUGGESTED RETAIL PRICE OF THIS MODEL: $
	OPTIONAL EQUIPMENT INSTALLED ON THIS VEHICLE BY MANUFACTURER
	OPTION # DESCRIPTION

	OPTIONS SUBTOTAL	
	VEHICLE TOTAL	
	DESTINATION CHARGE	
	DEALER PREP	
	OTHER	
	TOTAL AMOUNT	$

brochure for every model of the same brand. Don't get confused between models. What is standard on one model may not be standard on another. Most manufacturers will designate a model change if the standard equipment changes. Standard equipment cannot usually be removed for special orders. Most good manufacturers will show a base price for each model. This base MSRP includes all the standard equipment. It does not include optional equipment.

On the right side of the sheet you will find a list of optional equipment installed by the manufacturer. A dealer can change the optional equipment for stock items or special orders. Some manufacturers have 'standard runs' that include specific optional equipment unless a request is received from a dealer for an addition or deletion. For example: a standard run may include a spare tire, but a dealer who wants a 'special' for a show or promotion could exclude the spare from a number of units. Most buyers would not notice the omission when comparing prices with a competitor. You must, therefore, be very careful when comparing optional equipment.

An easy way to overcome

Honey, look here. The man said that the bypass valve was optional but here it is on the standard equipment list. I think he was trying to cheat us.

manipulation of optional equipment is to look at the box shown as 'options subtotal'. Any difference in the list will be reflected in the dollar figure in this box. Genuine MSRP sheets are designed so you can get a consistent value for the 'vehicle total' amount. This is the figure you must compare when working with two or more dealers for the same model.

You can't do much about the destination charge unless it's inflated, but watch out for the "dealer prep". This is usually a bonus amount for the dealer. Disregard it in all computations unless something special has been done to the RV at the dealership. If so, demand to know what was done and find out whether it's an excuse to inflate the figure.

The vehicle total price is very important for negotiations when buy-day arrives. It will tell you how much to expect as an allowance for a trade-in or how much you should receive as a discount. The vehicle total figure is based on a multiplying factor from manufacturing cost figures. It is possible for the multiplying factor to change from plant to plant or to adjust for inflation and other costs. Usually, however, variations in this figure are negligible.

You should also note that the manufacturing plant is shown on the MSRP sheet. The location of the plant will tell you if the transportation charge is legitimate. (Charge should be $1 per mile **maximum**.)

Getting a genuine MSRP sheet is paramount. Most are two colors. Good manufacturers produce one computer-generated two-color MSRP sheet for each motor home or travel trailer built. Do not negotiate with any dealer who refuses to give you a copy of the MSRP sheet or order form with list prices. You can make adequate comparisons with either one.

How do I compare one RV brand with another — especially if I decide to go used?

To buy a used RV, you'll need to visit at least five dealerships to get a good feel for brand and floor plan availability. You'll have to leave your telephone number with any salesperson interested in future business. Most will use a card filing system to keep in touch. The good salespeople will call you as soon as anything comes in that fits your basic requirements. Most, however, will never call you.

If you are considering an RV not older than five years, you should compare with new models. Begin by using MSRP sheets and advertised prices as a basis for the real value of the purchase. You should keep brochures and MSRP sheets just as if you were going to buy new. I can't begin to tell you the number of RVers who have paid as much (and sometimes more) for a used RV as the price of a new one.

Smoothy knows how to apply the pressure on an exceptional used RV. He will say, *"There's not another one exactly like it anywhere."* He'll be right, of course. Every used RV is unique because of the wear and tear factor. This doesn't mean,

Send us *The RV Rating Book*!

however, that you should rush into buying the first decent used RV you find. Extensive shopping is still a priority. The old adage 'there's always another fish' applies as much to RVs as to anything else. Don't let Smoothy hook you.

If you decide to buy an RV over five years old, go primarily by brand and condition. You need to keep quality the big priority. Later on we'll get into appraising — something you'll want to learn.

When buying used, you'll compare prices and condition through your notes. Don't expect to remember everything. Most of us remember three things — then we're lost. You may do better than the average, but you'll save a lot of money by using pencil and paper.

There's a danger in trusting a salesperson's opinion on used RVs because the profits are usually larger than new. After you look at twenty or thirty used RVs, you're almost ready for anything that looks good. Don't be fooled into accepting too many compromises.

How about buying from a private party?

You can get a very good buy from a private party, but use the same techniques as buying from a dealer. Do the dealer route first. After you get past a number of dealers, you may be interested in starting a search for a private party sale; but consider the following: 1) Many of these sellers have had plenty of experience handling people, they have a sense of the market, and they know that many buyers don't trust dealers. 2) When you buy from an individual, you have almost no recourse once you pay. It's usually a pure 'buyer beware' situation. 3) The private party is usually in love with the RV even if they don't know its real condition and value. They get their figures from the newspaper or from the asking price of the local dealer.

I've seen as many people get ripped off by private owners as by dealers. If you don't follow the same basic procedure as buying from a dealer, your dollars will be in mortal danger.

This is our regular price, but right now it's on special.

This simple statement, and many variations thereof, has moved enough RVs off the sales lots to circle the globe. We have, unfortunately, a learned reflex of listening more intently when we hear the words *save*, *discount*, or *special*. Smoothy has also learned to use these words after he gets a buying signal from you. You say *"This is nice,"* and he'll say something with the words *discount*, *save*, or *special*. Listen for them — but don't bite!

Rule 4

Don't trust the salesperson until he or she earns it

I do not wish to imply that the bulk of RV salespeople are not trustworthy. To the contrary, most RV salespeople want to give you good service while making a reasonable living. It's the American way. Of all the salespeople I've met, most of them want to be considered as good, solid citizens.

As you begin your search, you should listen carefully to each salesperson. You should be aware that he or she is trying hard to get your trust. Getting trust quickly is the "in thing" for RV dealerships. RV salespeople are encouraged to qualify, present, and close as quickly as possible. Their pay depends upon the close. They learn manipulative techniques to get you to that point. Even the most conscientious salesperson will manipulate a prospect. It's his duty. It's what the boss demands of him. The problem, however, is that manipulation destroys trust.

When you cut off any chance of closing today, most salespeople will lose interest. It's a natural state of the business. Don't write a salesperson off just because he or she won't spend hours with you on your search. Don't be totally unfair.

You should not feel obligated to ask for a particular salesperson on a second or third visit. Unless you feel strongly inclined, take whoever comes along. If the salesperson asks if you've been working with someone else, say, *"I've been talking to _____ , but you're okay with me."* Leave it there. They'll work it out.

The value of information collected from salespeople depends upon the accuracy — and honesty — of their spoken words. Make notes, then rate each salesperson on a scale of 1 to 10 — just like you would an RV. This rating will come in handy when you're ready to deal seriously.

How do RV salespeople qualify a buyer?

Each salesperson qualifies differently. The way they're supposed to do it is to ask you some 'when', 'what', and 'how' questions upfront. Most aren't that good at it. They generally stumble through the process by looking at the way you're dressed, the condition of the vehicle you're driving, or by what you incidentally tell them. Some don't qualify until they get into a presentation — if they get that far. A few will be precise.

The 'quick' qualifier...

misuses the system.

They are the professionals. You'll get a sense they've had some sales experience even if they don't know much about RVs.

Expect to be looked over even if not looked at. A real Smoothy will push hard for information by the time you get to the first RV. Somehow he'll find out if there's an urgency and then he'll go for your budget. His mind will be working fast. He may give you ten minutes if there's a chance that you're a 'hot' prospect.

Smoothy is always looking for a 'lay-down'. He wants the ones he can manipulate. He knows that 3 out of 10 RV buyers are 'easy-sells'. If you find yourself being dumped within fifteen minutes, you may have found a Smoothy — and he may have found that you are too tough.

If the salesperson sticks with you after you've convinced

him you're a serious buyer, expect the qualifying to continue. You should get probing questions about lifestyle and past preferences in RVs. Under no circumstances give your social security number or credit information at this time.

What is a trial close?

A trial close is the salesperson's test of your resistance to closing (signing the contract). For example, you say, *"I like it,"* and he immediately pushes the urgency issue. He may even try to get you to the office to work on the figures. A professional salesperson will look for buying signals, so you must avoid offhand remarks about exceptional features. Some RV buyers get so emotional that the buying signals never stop.

Buying signals will stop a good presentation. When the signal is given, a salesperson will probably try to get you into a closing situation. When it doesn't work, he'll start over but the presentation might lose something in the meantime. If you nod too many times, he'll make a move like, *"Would $300 a month be about right?"* or *"Let's see what we can work out in figures."* Trial closes are exciting for a professional salesperson because it's a test of qualifying, gaining trust, and manipulation. It's all designed to get you to the desk.

What is a 'turn'?

A 'turn' is a technique of passing you to another salesperson or the sales manager. This procedure is often required at auto dealerships and has found its way into many RV dealerships. In many ways, it's required because of weaknesses in the system. If the salesperson has good qualifying and follow-up techniques, the turn shouldn't be necessary.

Because RV selling often lacks professionalism, you may find the turn an interesting aspect of your RV shopping. Be aware that the 'turn' is often made to another salesperson with a false title. Usually this is obvious. If the 'turn' is to a real sales manager, be cordial — get as much information as you can. The sales manager is often the most informed person on the staff.

When you've had enough, emphasize that you must leave. Don't get caught with flapping lips. Keep the plan going.

When and how do I control the leaving?

Keep it simple! *"I have to go,"* works fine. Don't put a time limit too early into the session. If the salesperson is getting into a presentation, take advantage of it. Don't rush off. Get all you can when you can.

A good salesperson will not let you go until you make a trip to the office. *"Let's load you down with brochures,"* is a statement that should work for him. When in the office, he might try, *"While you're here, how about some figures?"* You'll find it hard to stay away from the salesperson's desk. If you find yourself there, spend time with the brochures. Watch out for hard-sell tactics. Because every salesperson should be proficient in getting you to his desk, you have to be ready to apply the brakes. Since most salespeople won't give you much for figures if you aren't buying <u>today</u>, take your brochure and run.

Don't forget. . .

**these things could
happen to you.**

Don't worry about the high mileage. The rental company had a big service department and changed oil every 2,000 miles.

When Smoothy said this, he didn't know whether it was true or not. He said it because it sounded like the right thing to say to overcome an objection. If you want to have fun being a *Perry Mason*, look the salesperson in the face and ask a couple of those prepared questions when a statement of this nature is made. The answers should help you determine if this person is worth your time.

Rule 5

Expect a good presentation of each RV shown

A presentation is an exposure of the features and benefits of a product or service. A good RV salesperson will take you through a presentation in a manner adjusted in time and intensity to your needs.

Always ask for a brochure before the presentation begins. By now you know that the brochure is important, but from now on you're going to learn that it's an indispensable tool for a good buy.

If the salesperson begins by making an organized presentation, let him lead. If the presentation is poorly performed, take over — lead the way by asking questions. Either way, make notes in the brochure of interesting features and quoted prices.

A good presentation will include positive statements about the features (i.e. the rubber roof, the enclosed propane bottles, the special suspension) and statements about the benefit of those features (example: *"The rubber roof's insulation and noise reduction abilities will make living in the RV more comfortable."*). Lazy salespeople won't do this because it takes rehearsing and study.

The presentation should be considered as your reward for visiting a dealership. Do not accept a simple tour of the inventory. If explanations are not given and questions are not completely answered, you should wipe the salesperson from your list of candidates for buy-day.

In case you have to control the presentation, you should have an organized plan. You should prepare to lead the salesperson around the RV while asking about construction features. Prepare to ask questions about the roof. Dress casually so that you can easily study the suspension. Have questions ready about the axles, rails, and tires. You will, in actuality, be conducting an

Nice wood!

appraisal of the RV—a subject covered extensively in *The Language of RVing.*

A touch tight!

Inside, you will check the galley (kitchen) first then the bathroom and the bedroom. Look at the cabinetry and the fixtures. Study the cabinet cuts. Drawers are very important. Quality of material and workmanship must be noted. Look into corners and under cushions. When you get to the bathroom, plan on spending a few minutes studying the seams around the shower. Is it a real shower (fiberglass or ABS walls) or an imitation shower (vinyl walls)? If you plan on using the shower often, you won't want anything except a high quality wraparound stall. If you spend

It may be too short.

most of your inspection time in the galley and bathroom, you'll soon begin to get the big picture on overall quality. (See 'galley' in *The Language of RVing*.)

Whether the salesperson leads or you lead, don't get shortchanged. A presentation, a brochure, and *The RV Rating Book* are requirements for a good buying decision.

How do I ask for a presentation?

Be bold! An organized presentation is the essence of the sales process. Whether or not a salesperson can properly qualify or close, he must be able to intelligently talk about the product. *"Will you tell me about this brand?"* should be enough to get a presenta-tion going. Of my students who have gone on a serious shopping campaign, less than 10% have been able to get a good presentation. They report having to lead the salesperson by asking pertinent questions. Be-cause of these low percent-

ages, you'll have to get what you can when you can.

If you come across an experienced salesperson, allow him or her to go through the complete presentation with minimum interruptions. Don't give buying signals. Keep busy taking notes. A good salesperson likes the attention given by a prospect. If he tries to rush through the presentation, you may have to question him to slow him down.

What is a good RV presentation?

A good presentation is well practiced — just like putting on a staged affair. If the presenter is skillful, he'll get into the details smoothly. In the first place, he'll be sure that a complete presentation is made only on an RV in which you have interest. I recommend that an RV salesperson have two presentations ready: a shopper presentation and a buyer presentation.

The shopper presentation, if performed correctly, will get into particulars about the manufacturer, the brand, and general construction. On an RV, this should take about five minutes. It will cover all points in an organized manner. The presenter should begin near the front where you can see the name and the profile as he points to important structural and design characteristics. He'll then take you inside where he'll talk about features and benefits distinct to the brand — not any particular model. After about five minutes, he should encourage you to ask questions.

Let me show you the new features with benefits.

A good presenter will know when to stop talking and begin looking for buying signals. If the interest in the particular RV is genuine, he may ask you if you have the time for a complete presentation. If you indicate you don't have the time, a good salesperson will immediately try to get an appointment. If rapport has been established, you will probably go for this approach.

If you show serious interest in a particular RV or brand, a professional salesperson will attempt to take you through a complete buyer presentation. With RVs this takes between

Notice the floor is attached to the frame every four inches so you won't feel the road bumps in your feet.

twenty and thirty minutes. If the presentation is too short, something will have been left out. If it's too long, you will get weary and the salesperson will feel rushed to get you into a closing situation. An effective buyer presentation begins with qualifying. If you are primarily destined for a motor home, a complete presentation on a travel trailer would be a waste of time.

Listen carefully to the presenter. If he gets talking too fast, slow him down so you don't miss anything. Keep your spouse with you. Both of you must give the presenter full attention. This is simple courtesy. A presentation of any product is a serious act.

After the presentation, take a moment to go over your notes with the salesperson. He might have valuable insights that are relevant and helpful. If he's been in RV sales for over five years, his comments should have some value.

How do I check out an RV on my own?

Because of the difficulty of getting a good presentation on an RV, you're going to be prepared to check it out all by yourself. It's quite easy and can be fun. In most cases, you should ask the salesperson for permission. If you do it right, he'll get the point and leave you alone.

You'll need your brochure in hand. Don't inspect an RV without it. A well-designed brochure will illustrate every feature the manufacturer can muster (who should know better than the manufacturer?). The manufacturers have spent hundreds of hours and thousands of dollars to put this booklet into your hand. They've given you their building secrets. They've dissected the competition to make their product's distinguishing features stand out. Even with all this work, most brochures will go to waste. Yours won't. You're going to use it as a guide to check out the real product.

There should be two or three pages in the brochure that cover construction features. Some will even get into the techniques and philosophy of build. This information is worth its weight in gold. The task at hand is for you to compare these illustrations and specifications with those you see in the real model.

Do your walk-around by the numbers as follows: 1) exterior walls, 2) roof, 3) frame and suspension, 4) floor, 5) cabinets, 6) interior walls, 7) windows, 8) bath, 9) appliances, and 10) furnishings. It'll work if you stick with it. I ask my students to score each area from 1 to 10. It'll take you a while to get into this; but you should be able to do well after a few trial runs. Your comments in each area are important, so be as complete as possible. This is your review information. This is what you'll use at home to make your decision.

During your walk-around, look for interesting features and deficiencies. Think of it as competition in a game or a sport. You are out to win. You're out to overpower the glitter makers for your dollars and your future. Whether you are with a salesperson or alone, you will need to fight for control. You will need to lift, poke, touch, and smell. If you make it a habit, it will stay with you every time you enter an RV. When you

RV Rating Chart

Scoring
10 — Excellent
9 — Very good
8 — Good
7 — Good with reservations
6 — Fair
5 — Poor
4 — Not acceptable
3 — Seriously flawed
2 — Extremely flawed
1 — Total disaster

sit at home, you'll remember in the same order you used when you inspected the real thing. You'll soon begin to feel confident that your 5-year plan will be more than a dream — it will be a vision of your adventures to come.

One at a time

Exterior Walls	4
Roof	___
Frame and Suspension	___
Floor	___
Cabinets	___
Interior Walls	___
Windows	___
Bath	___
Appliances	___
Furnishings	___

Those compartment seals look like they came from a dime store. I'll give it a 4.

This is the state-of-the-art in RVs. It has the best in structure and insulation.

This statement was made by a salesperson who knew the RV being shown was below entry level. It was being shown to a little old lady who wanted to live alone on relatives' property.

Smoothy is quick to judge the knowledge and naivete of the prospect. His words are his weapons when he moves in for the kill. Like a military tank, Smoothy has but one purpose.

Rule 6

Go for the quality!

It's important to remember that quality and brand are not necessarily synonymous. Many brands have had severe changes in building characteristics because the brand name changed ownership. Some of these brands have been reduced in quality. Some have been upgraded. When looking for a new RV, you can usually judge brands as being consistent only for a particular year. If looking for used, you'll have to be very careful.

At this point you should be ready to choose a brand and an alternate. You should have established a budget and know which brands will fit that budget. If you need to adjust your budget later, you may have to switch from new to used. If you go used, it might be practical to consider from three to five brands. All the knowledge and notes you have collected will be very important if you go this route.

The average RV buyer ignores brands because he's been told that the differences are minor. The RV industry has been careful not to be critical of the competition because every manufacturer knows how vulnerable its own brands are. RV manufacturing is profitable because of consumer ignorance — and some manufacturers want to keep it that way.

You should, of course, study *The RV Rating Book.* It will give you the ratings of each model of most brands. As you get into the process, keep an open mind. It's easy to get caught in glitter and floor plan. It's easy to rationalize buying lower quality. It's easy to accept pleasing yourself or another in spite of the facts. Your goal should be to hit the road with your RV as a good investment — not just an expenditure.

How do I know that the brand is good?

By now you should know the importance of good presentations and of your own appraisals. If you follow the first six rules of this book, you will eliminate 50% of the brands on the market.

I like to have my students start their appraisals with the roof and the galley. By checking the roof for quality of workmanship and materials, you'll get a good picture of what's under the skin. If you see flaws on the exterior, especially the roof, you can bet there are even more deficiencies you can't see without taking the RV apart.

We have a sign in our conference room that says, *"The manufacturer who can't build a good galley can't build a good RV."* This statement has been reinforced time and time again

Good galleys or bust!

We want good RVs

by data and comments put into our computer's memory banks. There is no question at RV Consumer Group that if the galley is designed for vacation use, the rest of the RV is built for vacation use. This doesn't mean the quality is poor; it means the quality is adequate for vacation use — not snowbirding or fulltiming. This difference is important.

Long ago I discounted the flat one-piece aluminum roof as being so deficient in long-life qualities that I downgrade every RV with this type of roof. Whether the aluminum has no backing or hardbacking makes little difference to me. The philosophy of any manufacturer who uses this roof material is always in question. They know this type of material is not forgiving to workmanship or maintenance deficiencies. They know that for a few bucks more they can do better. They also know that 75% of the RV buying public is ignorant of this roof's tendency to leak. It's all tied up in the big game of marketing and profit.

So in the short of it, you can't know that a brand is good beyond the model year on which you're working. There is absolutely no sure way of knowing if a particular unit is good even though the brand's rating is high. Lemons happen, and some factories produce more lemons than others. Choosing a manufacturer who has a reputation for sloppy workmanship means more chances of buying a lemon. By going for quality in workmanship you're betting that a consistently good brand in the past will be a good brand today.

How far down do I settle for less?

It all gets down to bravery. If you feel secure in risking thousands of dollars on looks, go for whatever looks good to you. If, however, you buy an RV rated below 60 in *The RV Rating Book*, I think you are asking for lots of frustration when you hit the road.

Don't gamble...

on quality!

I personally don't want to be bothered by junk at my stage of life. I don't need a gold-plated RV, but I want substance. I've found out there's rarely a reason to drop in quality.

What do I say to a relative or friend who has one of *those?*

Having a neighbor, relative, or friend show up with an RV that you have learned is not of acceptable quality puts you in a tough spot. Once they find out that you're in the upper 10% of the world in RV knowledge (which you will be by the time you finish this book) they will, sooner or later, ask for your opinion. Because almost everyone is defensive of their actions when it comes to spending money, even if they complain, watch out. If you want to keep these people as friends, you better say little. Show them you care by buying them a copy of this book. They might believe me quicker than they'll believe you. Absolutely do not bring up the issue. Don't lose friendship to prove a point.

Every RVer has the responsibility of spreading information about RVing. To get the point across use short phrases like:

➤ *"All RVs are not created equal."*
➤ *"A good RV begins with a good roof and superb galley."*
➤ *"RVs should last twenty years without major failure."*

When you spread this kind of information, you'll sleep well knowing you have given your friends insights towards making the right choices.

This is the best buy for the money!

Smoothy said this about a brand rated below 60 in *The RV Rating Book*. Smoothy says it so often in one way or another that it sounds convincing. There's no hesitation, eye shifting, or stammer. He waits for a buying signal — then POW!

Smoothy is an expert at shifting gears. He'll work the trust game. He'll play the *take it or leave it* game. If he sees a weakness, he might go for the throat almost immediately.

Rule 7

Choose two dealerships for new and five dealerships for used

The smart RV buyer begins with the local dealerships and gives those dealerships the benefit of the doubt. You, as a smart RV buyer, will communicate by visits and by phone. You will get to know the management. If, however, the dealership does not have acceptable brands, you will drop it like a hot potato.

Beware of dealerships that are considered regional discount houses. Although these dealerships usually have some good brands, they also have hot-shot salespeople. Regional discount houses work beyond their communities. They bring buyers in — and close them today. You will probably have a tough time getting good information at an RV discount house.

By now you should have made your decision on type, size, and price range. You should be working hard on brand and floor plan. Choosing dealerships and salespeople with whom you can work is very important at this time. You will need rapport with the salesperson if you want to get the best deal possible. A good salesperson will represent the dealership while caring about your needs.

If you are buying used, be sure you understand the complications and techniques we are discussing in this section. Because any dealer can take in any type, size, brand, or floor plan as a trade, you need to be listed with as many dealerships as practical. Whether you buy new or used, what you're after is the best RV you can buy for the money you have budgeted.

Is it right to work one dealership against the other?

Oh yes! It's an old game of skirmishes. They work you — you work them. Even though you have the advantage, they have the record for winning. They are not, of course, going to win this battle. By now, you understand the importance of control and direction. You're going to keep your eye on the 5-year plan as you control visits, time, and the pen. If you get out of control, Smoothy will win — and you know it.

By now you have a file full of brochures and accurate figures from the five dealerships you've been visiting. You have already chosen type and size and are narrowing it to two brands. You have a close idea of your floor plan, and you'll have worked your budget to within 10%. By this time you'll be loaded with copies of MSRP sheets and worksheets for brands and models you are considering. You'll have *The RV Rating Book under your arm.* You have the power in your hands to take control of buy-day.

As you visit one of the two dealerships you've chosen for the buy, you may or may not have chosen the person with whom you'll negotiate. This is not really important unless you've found that exceptional salesperson. Since you probably know exactly what you're after, the visits to the dealerships from now on are primarily to get the final figures for study.

Tell the salesperson your timetable. Tell him that you're making a decision soon and that he's competing with another dealer. Do not, and I repeat, do not tell the salesperson which other dealership you are considering. If the salesperson knows the other dealership's sales philosophy, he'll know how to work you. Keep him guessing. Tell him what brand and model you're considering. If it requires a special order, you'll need to get accurate specifics at this time. Find out the location of the manufacturing plant. (It should be on the MSRP sheet, but double check anyway.)

On this last visit before you decide which dealer to try, you may want to get any final advice the salesperson can give. Listen intently. If he thinks you're still wavering, he'll work hard to get your trust. A salesperson may hold back giving advice if he thinks the prospect is inflexible. Even though he may know something you don't about other models or equipment, he may be reluctant to advise you for fear of losing whatever he has going. Show your interest by listening. It's your last chance before buy-day.

The ball game changes a bit if you're going for used. With used you have to be ready to deal the day you look. Like new, however, you should know what you want and what compromises you're willing to make. The big difference will be that you can't order another just like it.

If you get excited over a used RV, try for a 3-day $100 refundable hold. This will give you time to check further and to think a bit. The value of a hold, however, depends much on the dealership. Some dealerships will limit holds to a shorter time and may require a firmer commitment. The dealer's reputation for honoring a hold is very important when buying used. You need to be aware that some dealers use the hold to push the next prospect on the same vehicle for a quick sale at a higher profit. (See 'subject to...' in *The Language of RVing.*)

Whether buying new or used, be honest about your time-table and needs. Work hard at getting the salesperson excited about working with you on the purchase. If the salesperson says, *"I'll beat anybody's price,"* you know you are beginning to get control of buy-day.

What about those telephone calls?

You'll be kept busy on the phone. Be polite, be brief, be honest, and don't blab! Set a maximum of ten minutes for any call. Make the salesperson call back if necessary. If you have a real Smoothy, he'll promise you anything to get you to his desk. Some sales-people aren't good on the phone. Some are gabby — don't waste your time with these. Use the telephone to your advantage by

Yes, I'm looking at the inventory right now. We have exactly what you want.

qualifying the salesperson. It's a great reverse play. If you come to the conclusion that you don't want a particular salesperson to call again, say so. If you've made up your mind to buy from another dealer, be honest and say so. By being honest, you might get some fascinating figures.

If you promise to go to the dealership for any reason, don't make an appointment unless you intend to keep it. A good salesperson will work his butt off for a forthright buyer. I've seen some tremendous deals because the salesperson worked the sales manager into going for less profit.

What do I do with the salesperson who turns me off at a dealership that otherwise seems good?

Call the dealership until you find a salesperson with whom you think you can work. Make an appointment. If seen by the other salesperson, acknowledge only with a slight nod or smile. Do not encourage the other salesperson to interfere. Snub him if necessary. If queried by the new salesperson about the other, simply say, *"You're doing fine."* Do not get involved in a discussion on commission splits or say anything negative about the other salesperson. Let them hash it out.

What do you mean you don't want me as your salesperson? I'm the only one here that knows anything!

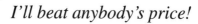

I'll beat anybody's price!

This is probably one of the few things you should be happy to hear Smoothy say. It opens the door for a discussion of prices. It gives you a chance to pin him down and make him sweat.

Don't let Smoothy forget that he said those four **big** words.

Rule 8

Have all your facts on paper

You can't make a good buy without some information on paper. The more you have, the stronger your chances of getting within 2% of the best deal possible. Most people ignore collecting information because it takes time and effort. I learned over a 40-year span that savings in time and money were proportional to the habit of collecting information at each step of the way. That's the way it works for me, and it can do the same for you.

When you visit a dealership, you should have plenty of ammunition in a closed folder or small case. You should have a brochure for every RV you are considering. You should have the MSRP sheet if new or the average book retail if used. You should have *The RV Rating Book*'s highway safety, durability, and value ratings marked in bold numbers on the cover of every brochure.

If you have a trade, know the appraisal book wholesale and retail figures. When you know the ACV (Actual Cash Value) of your trade, you can figure how much to expect as an allowance on another RV. Most RV buyers lose money because they don't know how to figure their trade into the deal.

There is nothing that will keep a salesperson on his or her toes like a buyer loaded for bear. A good salesperson will accept it as a challenge — knowing the profit may be minimal but the prize is still worth going after. When you have the information in hand, you will gain respect — and you will deserve it.

How do I get realistic used RV values?

If you are buying used, have a trade-in, or are trying to figure depreciation factors for the brand you are considering, you will need to use two appraisal books — N.A.D.A. and Kelley Blue Book. You can usually find these books at the library, bank, credit union, or get the figures through RV Consumer Group. I recommend averaging from both books since both use nationwide subscriber input to determine the values.

Most dealers use both books. Smart salespeople know how to use appraisal books to their advantage. For example: If the customer asks to see the book value on an RV being considered, the salesperson will show the book with the highest value. Of course, he will do the opposite for trade-ins. Some dealers also use outdated books to their advantage. Always check the months and year on the book cover. Ask for copies of the applicable pages. If you can't get copies, make notes of the values. Dealers make plenty of money on trades because most RV buyers are ignorant of trade values. I have seen hundreds of RV buyers make seemingly good deals until further checking showed the trade was practically given away. Knowing the value of your trade will save you thousands of dollars — an incentive that should make you work harder for buy-day.

An appraisal book will give you the following data: 1) the original MSRP <u>base</u> price (suggested list when <u>new</u>), 2) the used wholesale, 3) the used retail, 4) optional equipment values, and 5) a mileage schedule for motor homes. You will need all five of these values. Keep in mind that optional equipment values are overrated by the dealer when selling and underrated when figuring trade-in allowances. Optional equipment does not include any item that is standard equipment when new. If you average the figures from both books, you should have a good beginning for ACV. You will also need to add or subtract for the condition and for any reduced demand of a particular type, model, or floor plan in your section of the country. I recommend no more than 20% for pluses, but there's no limit on negatives.

Most salespeople cannot appraise accurately. For this reason, you may find big variations in used values among dealers. We have found great used RV values at dealerships because a trade was brought in low. On the other side of the picture, you'll find many used RV prices out-of-sight because the dealer allowed too much. The unlucky buyer is the one who thinks all prices are fair. You don't. Your plan is to buy low and trade high.

How important is the warranty?

A warranty is very important because it separates the good, well-established manufacturers from all others. Without warranty facts in your hand, you don't know what the warranty is. Manufacturers like Fleetwood, Winnebago, Carriage, and Holiday Rambler will furnish complete warranty details on request. Get them and study them.

Smaller manufacturers may have a good warranty on their products if you can find a service center to do the work. These details have to be considered. If you buy from one of these smaller companies, talk with the factory. Most have a toll-free number. Have them mail you details. Don't cross off small manufacturers because they have a hundred or less dealerships. These are often the best RVs for the money. Having warranty details in your hand before buy-day is only common sense.

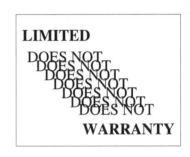

Study the fine print.

Now that I'm ready to buy, what information do I need to take with me to the dealership?

Since the final step in the buying decision has to do with budget and price, the time has come to have your facts and figures on paper. You should have copies of the MSRP sheets if buying new; and if buying used, you should know the wholesale and retail values. If you have a trade, you'll also want to know its wholesale and retail values.

If you have a worksheet that lists special equipment and services, you'll need it close at hand. Review it at home and be sure it's all clear in your mind. Good salespeople have a great skill for confusing an anxious buyer. As I mentioned before, getting down to within 2% of the very bottom goes beyond skirmishing — it's warfare.

Play it smart!

Since this one will give me more for the trade, I'll take it instead of...

Don't leave home without a brochure of the exact unit for which you'll be negotiating and two of the competition's brochures. The competition's brochures are shake-up devices. Any figures you have from the competition should be in your billfold so they don't accidently fall into the salesperson's hands. It's your secret weapon.

Don't forget your trade-in's title or registration. If you have a payoff, get the figure for approximately ten days after you plan on closing the deal. Don't expect the salesperson to get the payoff for you. He can do it, but it adds another unnecessary variable to the negotiations.

If you've had your trade appraised, or if you've had a cash offer, keep those figures hidden but handy. You need to know them, but it might be to your advantage that the salesperson doesn't know them.

As you prepare these papers for buy-day, think of how much 1% of the <u>retail value</u> will save you in the long run. Each $100 saved will represent about $200 in real savings over a 10-year financing span. Money saved now will improve the quality of those great adventures on your horizon.

Is there an easy way to get a close estimate of payments?

For some it's easy. For some working with figures is never easy. I think, however, that anyone who is willing to venture onto our massive and busy highway system with an RV will be able to conquer a simple formula.

You'll need to do some checking on your own for the best current interest rates. As you call each financial institution, get the interest rate and the monthly payment for each $100 financed for the financing term. Since most RVs are sold on a 120 month (10-year) term, you should include that term and one longer or shorter term. This monthly payment for each $100 will make it easy for you to double-check with any figure the dealership gives you.

Let's say the amount you are financing is $10,000. If the bank tells you that your monthly payment is $1.50 for each $100 for a specific term, simply take the last two figures off the finance amount and multiply by $1.50. You can see that your payment for that term with a balance of $10,000 would be $150. Put the information with the name of the bank on a small card. You now have a figure that will put you in control of this part of the negotiations — while keeping you in budget.

Don't lose sight of type and budget.

This RV has a special price because we've made a deal with the manufacturer to buy a large number of units.

Although possible, it's rarely the case. When Smoothy said this, one manufacturer had discounted a small number of discontinued models. Smoothy exaggerated the purchase in advertising and to prospects.

This tactic must work because Smoothy uses it time and again.

Rule 9

Be prepared to walk away

Buy-day has arrived. You've cased the business several times and are now ready for action. You have your arsenal of weapons and have girded yourself with the best armor you can accumulate. You are as ready.

Even as you enter the dealership, you must have a willingness to walk away if anything doesn't feel right. You know that you have an easy way to escape — just get on your feet and make them move.

If you find you need thinking space during the negotiations, take it. If you need a cup of coffee to slow down the pace, go to the local restaurant. If your stomach doesn't feel right, don't take antiacid — take a hike.

You must realize that even if you decide to walk away, a good salesperson will have techniques designed to stop you. Some salespeople will stop you before you hit the door. One of our ex-car salesman students had a successful technique of stopping a walkaway prospect in mid-stride with a big, "Say!". It was then back to the table to start over. A true Smoothy loves the challenge of bringing you back. He's an expert. You're the novice.

You, however, will be trained to handle the situation. You'll simply turn and say, "We'll see," then leave. The salesperson has your phone number and you have notes. It'll be a draw for now.

If you really want a particular RV and need it now, don't allow the salesperson to know it. Make him or her sweat. Sit in your vehicle a few minutes. It's a poker game. It's now your skill against the skill of the house. If you decide to go back to the desk, do not start over. Continue from where you left off with a review of the facts and figures.

Walking away can save you money. How far you walk depends on the urgency for that particular RV. If the salesperson knows of the urgency, the road will be bumpy. Although there are always too many variables for absolutes, the best way to walk is to go all the way. There's always a tomorrow.

Isn't the 5-year plan difficult to keep in focus during the pressure of negotiating?

Anxiety at the closing desk is normal. If you are anxious because you are making an important decision, that's good. If you are simply anxious to get into your new RV, that's bad. Impatience is what the salesperson will look for as a sign of weakness. If your salesperson is a Smoothy, any impatience could cost you between 2% and 5% of the retail value. On buy-day you need to know where you are now and where you're going.

It's time to breathe deep and go slow. If you are married, your spouse should be with you and both should have agreed on all fundamentals before buy-day. If there is any serious disagreement at the dealership, it's best to go home and start over. If the salesperson sees contention, he knows he must overcome the objection and lock it up solid. He knows that every skill he has acquired in sales has to be put into motion. His thoughts will be running one-way: *"This is the day to close this deal."*

If there is any question between you and your spouse about your choices, take a last look at your 5-year plan. Ask yourself the following questions: Does the type fit? Does the

size fit? Does the brand fit? Does the floor plan fit? Does the final price and payment fit? If you both agree with affirmative answers, then you are ready for buy-day. Let's do it!

How do I know when I'm being ripped off?

If you are entering a dealership with each of the previous 8 rules in place, you'll be safe within 5% of the best deal you can get. On buy-day, you'll be working on that 5%. How much of that 5% you can keep in your savings account will depend on your tenacity to protect every dollar you've accumulated through hard work. To be sure you know where you are, let's look at some percentages and figures.

The gross profit built into most MSRP sheets is between 28 and 32%. There's no way you're going to know the exact gross profit unless you see an invoice and know if there's a volume-bonus in the system. Because of the high cost of keeping an RV on the sales lot, most dealers want to hold a minimum of 15% gross profit. Some will quickly drop to a 12% profit. At the other extreme, I know a few dealers who will accept 8-10% gross profit. Always keep in mind that these profit figures are based on a genuine MSRP retail price. The dealer's personal pricing structure doesn't count.

Because very high percentages of RV buyers allow deal-ers to get a 20% gross profit, you will help balance the system by working hard to get the dealer to accept a 10% or less gross profit on your deal. Your goal on buy-day is to save dollars, so let's start off by expecting to pay a maximum of 80% of MSRP.

Your worksheet should go this way:

Full Retail:

MSRP	$25,000*
Add-on equipment and services	3,000
Total retail	28,000

Plus:

Freight or Transportation	400
Sales tax (5%)	1,400
License	100
Total price	**$29,900**

You pay:

80% of total retail	22,400
Plus freight.........................	400
Plus tax and license	1,500
plus payoff	1,000
less trade at ACV**	-5,500
Balance due	**$19,800**

*Always work from MSRP to avoid confusion.
** Actual Cash Value.

I can't afford to give you more than a 12% discount.

If you don't have a trade, it's really quite easy now that you have an idea of what discount you'll be working with from the figures in your folder. In the example given you know you're somewhere near the bottom. The dealer would now have a gross profit between $2,000 and $3,000 (or between 10% and 12%) without add-on equipment. How much he wants to hold depends on his business philosophy and how badly he wants to get rid of a stocked item. How much profit is built into the add-on equipment and services? It's probably somewhere between $1000 and $1500.

Forget MSRP. I'll give you 10% off the special price if you buy today.

If you have a trade, you should be looking at the ACV figure while the dealer is looking at the amount of profit he'll make when he retails the RV. If the deal is close you'll never know whether he actually considers the trade a plus or minus to the deal. It's in his mind. That's why you work with at least two dealers. They never think the same when it comes to ACV. They treat a trade as a cash outlay, so you need to think of it as a cash value or simply how much cash you can readily get for it on the open market. If you've done your homework, you know this figure. In the example, this is the $5,500 deducted after you subtract the cash discount from the retail price of $28,000.

Now that you have an idea of how to deal with the figures, you know you can have these figures ready on a worksheet of your own in your folder. Make the worksheet so that you understand it. If any serious questions surface during the negotiations, walk! There's always another day.

How do I handle the close?

The close is always pressure. The amount of pressure will depend on how well you've done your homework. A good salesperson will try to get you off your figures and into his.

Keep in mind that you will be fighting to save money and the salesperson will be fighting to keep as much of a commission as he can. If he's any good, he'll manipulate you somehow. You should be ready to put on the brakes or rev the engines — whatever the situation calls for. Remember, you're supposed to be in control.

Try to put the salesperson out of his comfort zone by negotiating in the RV. By taking the salesperson away from his desk, the telephone, and the sales manager, you will be taking some of his control. However, if you get him to accept your offer, <u>don't sign papers in the RV</u>. The final acceptance

Because selling is with us every day,

it's hard to turn and walk away.

of both parties must be done where you won't be distracted from studying the "fine print".

If you have a sharp salesperson, watch for the following techniques: 1) use of words, 2) pleasant conversation, 3) turning of the paperwork (contract) to you, 4) passing of the pen, 5) pleading look, 6) a touch of impatience, 7) "Time is now" attitude, 8) a resell of the features, 9) a resell on the price, and 10) putting pressure on the urgency factor. If the salesperson's adrenaline is flowing, he's in the best of form. This is the time to watch out.

You are now an expert buyer. Your adrenaline is flowing because you're ready for great adventures. You're thinking how every dollar saved here will take you that extra mile. You're not going to let any salesperson turn you into a robot. Victory is within your reach. Don't blow it!

Note from the author:

    If you'd like to know more about manipulative tactics of RV salespeople, get *How to Outwit Any Auto, Truck, or RV Dealer Every Time.* There's a special section in the back of the book titled *Dirty Tricks Glossary.* This is important for you to know because many RV dealers are now using auto dealer sales tactics.

> *Congratulations on your new trailer! To show our appreciation for the business, the sales manager has approved giving you a complete pre-delivery inspection for $75 instead of the regular price of $250.*

This one worked like a charm! I'd never heard it before and I'm not sure that Smoothy had ever tried it before. But since he picked up another $20 commission quick-like, I'm sure he'll try it again.

Of course, not everyone knows that most RV manufacturers pay for pre-delivery inspection. But now <u>you</u> do!

Rule 10

Prepare for back-end pressure

Back-end sales should not be an issue with most of you because few of you want these services or products. Big profits are made at RV dealerships from back-end sales. It's called back-end because they get the buyer in the back-end after the close — which the buyer thinks is the end. Back-end sales come from financing, insurance, extended warranties, and interior and exterior protection packages. Profits are so high in percentages that they are hard to compute. Profits from interest above the dealer buy-rate are often astronomical. Extended warranties are usually in the 50% gross profit area or higher. The list goes on, and the profits stay high.

The pressure exerted by dealer management for back-end sales is always high. The average back-end expert (called the finance manager, F & I officer, or business manager) earns between $50,000 and $100,000 a year. They are Smoothies of Smoothies. Compared to the average salesperson, BEE (back-end expert) is a real stinger.

You will never prepare enough for BEE if you've selected a high pressure dealership for buy-day. You can, however, make it a learning experience and walk away without it costing you. You can simply say "No!" to everything. You've come a long ways in learning to save thousands of dollars, so don't blow it now by letting your guard down.

In smaller neighborhood dealerships, the back-end services are often sold by the salesperson. In this scenario, it's easy to handle. If he finds you are reluctant, the salesperson won't jeopardize the sale by putting on too much pressure. Because the commissions are good, however, expect almost anything. All you need to say is "No!" and the subject should be dropped.

If you think you might consider an extended warranty,

payment insurance, or any RV interior or exterior coating protection, you should have inquired as to the cost and benefits during your research. If you wait until buy-day, you'll find the temptation as high as your urgency to hit the road. Do it before buy-day.

Are you saying that dealers make money on financing?

You bet your pretty monthly payments they do! Every RV dealer gets buy-rates from financial institutions. This buy-rate can be near prime. Any difference between the buy-rate and the interest rate charged on the contract will find itself in a trust account designated for the dealership. The details may be different with each financial institution, but the purpose of this system is to encourage dealers to work hard to get financing away from your own sources. Consider how much a dealer would make if the interest rate charged you is 10% and the dealer's buy rate is 8%. That 2% interest will be going to the dealer every month. At this percentage you can simply figure about 20% of the interest you pay will be going to the dealer. Do you want the dealer to get thousands of your hard-earned dollars for a few minutes of paperwork that should have been included in the deal? Of course not!

All this shows the importance of active research to get a good interest rate. Work the phone. Call all local banks. Call your credit union. Look in the paper for specials on interest rates. If you do this, you'll be prepared to negotiate when you're ushered into BEE's office. Work him to the <u>lowest</u> rate before you give him yours. BEE makes his living from getting a "Yes" from you. Be ready to fight BEE. If his stinger gets in, it's going to stay for years.

Keep in mind that these rules apply to autos and trucks. After all, that's where the RV industry learned to wheel and deal.

How do I know if I need payment protection insurance?

Usually payment insurance is too expensive for most of us. It is possible for older people to get good deals because there is no health check. If, for example, you are approaching 60, have a heart problem, are spending most of your money reserves on an RV, and your surviving spouse would have a hard time making the RV payments, you may want to consider a simple program. Unless you feel the odds are against your living through the financing term, go strictly for decreasing term. <u>Consider this only if your debt-to-income ratio is high and life expectancy is low</u>. To be sure, compare with regular insurance companies.

If you get confused about the cost, ask for accurate payment figures before the insurance is added and again after it's added. Be sure BEE gives you these figures in writing. Multiply the difference times the number of payments for the real cost. Other figures don't really count.

Know these things: BEE knows how to push. BEE knows how to scare. BEE works on anxiety and conscience. BEE comes across as a nice person. Often BEE will be a mother or grandfather type. BEE is always concerned for you. BEE gets your shields down. BEE always earns lots of money. BEE often functions on guile. BEE is always a Smoothy!

Oh yes! I remember the advice I gave to my wonderful children.

Sweet BEE

What about extended warranties?

Generally, extended warranties are not a good buy. Like payment protection, however, there is a scenario where an extended warranty may be worth considering. If you purchase

They want **what** figures?

Ask <u>before</u> you go in!

an almost new motor home which has had questionable care, if you are taking long voyages away from home, if you have no road-smarts, if your travel budget has been shot by the purchase, and if it makes you feel better even with the larger payment, an extended warranty might be worth considering. Otherwise, do not consider it a smart buy.

If you decide to consider an extended warranty, investigate the underwriter. Be absolutely clear what the policy <u>does not</u> cover. BEE is going to try very hard to sell you on this product. The commissions are big. A word of extreme caution: Most RV and auto buyers go in determined not to buy an extended warranty — but BEE makes the sting. Most buyers get it in the end.

What are the real costs of these 'back-end' services?

If you're having the purchase financed, double the quoted cost and you'll be pretty close to the real cost. If you're a cash buyer, figure how much you'd gain in interest over the normal financing term and add it to the quoted cost.

BEE will not want to do it, but get exact payments on the RV purchase before going into the 'business office'. As BEE gets done with each step, get new monthly payment figures <u>in writing</u>. Multiply the difference times the term. You'll soon see the real costs. And please, just because BEE seems to be a busy BEE, don't let him or her rush you. BEE is very astute. BEE is quick. Unlike RV salespeople, almost every BEE you meet will be a professional. There are few sloppy BEE's in the world. Beat BEE by practicing to say,

NO!

How do I know that I've gotten the best deal possible?

You don't. The important thing is that you've done the best you could and better than 90% of RV buyers world-wide.

When you leave the dealership, it's time to celebrate the adventure of buying an RV without getting ripped off. It's time to celebrate for the adventures that are just around the corner and over the next hill. It's time to move out — to hit the road.

We did it! We're within budget and we got what we want. **Let's hit the road!**

In closing . . .

I must emphasize that the attitude and performance of RV salespeople are the symptoms, not the cause, of a haphazard and often destructive demeanor towards the RV consumer. RV manufacturers are the cause of the condition. Their overall performance has been mediocre at best. At worst, manufacturers have performed with greed and profit as their only props while social conscience lay covered with dust just off stage. This attitude is infectious to those who sit in the audience.

RV manufacturers have an audience made up of retailers and their employees. This audience rarely throws tomatoes because its bread and butter comes from the manufacturers. Retailers know that their influence is minimal. The power is in the hands of the builders. Dealers sell what they get. They tell me they do what they must do to survive.

Once again I would like to quote from excerpts of my articles in *the RV Lookout.*

My experiences with RV manufacturers have been so depressing that it's difficult for me to think positively. I've seen so many people cheated out of a lifetime of accumulated assets that 'shocking' becomes an inadequate word. When you find unsophisticated and uncaring RV manufacturers making millions by marketing products with little substance, you must wonder about it all. I am probably not unlike the reporter who visits a starving nation and finds too few words to express the emotion that overshadows the task. I am not a radical — my Scottish blood keeps me from that extreme. I am not hard — my French blood keeps me tingling. I am just an RVer who loves the lifestyle.

The RV industry is in its infancy. It is now where the auto industry was in the early '30s — the decade of GM's beginning and Ford's Model A. No sense of social conscience has yet evolved from the hundreds of companies that are vying for market share in this very competitive atmosphere. It's like babes in the woods — babes of the Paul Bunyan size, large enough to destroy the forest. It's a time comparable to the gold rush days with an obvious difference — few of the participants are drowning, freezing to death, or dying from shoot-outs. Industry fatalities are low because the lack of available consumer information keeps profits high for the bad as well as for the good. This is a status quo protected. It shouldn't be this way. Good RV manufacturers should be bound by a sense of social conscience and mutual survival.

The American consumer is vengeful, however. We've proved time and again there's a limit to our patience. Although we've given the RV industry a bonanza of riches, they've thrown toys at our feet. We want more than toys. We want substance. We want RVs that will last. We want good products and fair dealings. We want the American RV industry to do for RVers what the

Japanese have done for the auto consumer. As RV consumers, we want fair treatment from those with whom we spend our savings. It's time for all of us to open our eyes to see beyond the next hill.

You can tell from your voyage through this book that I do not excuse RV dealers and salespeople for having an indifferent or belligerent attitude towards the RV consumer. I have shown you that you are vulnerable to their excesses of greed and for profit. RV dealers know that everything that I tell you is true although most will quickly declare, "Not me!"

You, as the consumer, have the power to put it right. You, as the consumer, can put unscrupulous RV dealers out of business in a very short time. You can do this by sticking to the ten rules in this book.

If you buy an RV with a determination to make it a good investment, you'll choose correctly. You'll begin with type and end with price. You won't let anyone turn this around. You'll stay on course and keep that $6,000 to improve your adventures.

You'll learn as you prepare questions to ask salespeople. You'll enjoy your new-found ability to interrogate as an expert. You won't be a real expert, of course, but you'll feel like one because you'll know more than most of those so-called experts you'll meet on your rounds.

As you leave the many dealerships you visited to get you started, you'll find yourself often vowing never to return. You'll begin to shake your head as you recognize line after line of bull and more bull. When you eliminate half the dealerships you will visit, you'll feel good about what you've learned and where you're going.

You won't get caught up in the trust game. You've learned enough to tread carefully when RV salespeople start spouting off about specials, sales, and discounts. You'll know what to expect when they start to put on the pressure. You'll have your escape plans tied to your feet — and you'll use them often.

You won't put up with a tour when a presentation is needed. You'll know how to ask. You'll know what to expect. If it doesn't go the way it should, you'll know how to lead. One way or another, you'll learn about the product.

By now you know enough to keep quality in focus. You'll associate brand with quality and have an idea which manufacturers are building acceptable RVs. You won't get overwhelmed by the many claims because you'll be past letting glitter cloud your eyesight.

You know that eventually you'll get down to choosing two dealerships for buy-day. When you get down to this number, you'll have the tools to work one against the other and not feel badly about doing it. You'll expect to save thousands of dollars and you'll know that it's your right to fight for the best deal you can get.

Your basic tools will be paper, pen, and *The RV Rating Book*. You'll combine these tools with brochures to build an arsenal that will take you to victory. You'll prepare a step at a time and then you'll give it your all. You'll know you're going to win.

When buy-day arrives, you'll be prepared to walk away if things aren't as they should be. You'll know that there's always a tomorrow. You'll take the time to review your preparation and check your 5-year plan. You won't let anyone rush you into a deal that's not to your advantage.

You will, of course, be prepared for back-end pressure. By

now you have a good picture of what to expect beyond the RV purchase. You'll know how to say "No!" and you'll remember how to use your feet. You won't let BEE rub his hands in glee after you leave the dealership.

There is more to learn than what is in this book, but what you have learned is a good beginning. If you follow the ten basic rules, you will save thousands of dollars and have a good chance of buying an RV that will fit into your 5-year plan. No system is guaranteed to keep Smoothy at bay, but having no system will most assuredly keep Smoothy richer and you poorer.

If you need help, remember that I and the rest of the staff of RV Consumer Group are here to help. You need not do it alone.

Happy trekking!

RV Consumer Group

is a nonprofit organization that

Rates RVs

 It is primarily operated by a staff of part-time and volunteer retired professionals.

 It has been conducting RV buying workshops and publishing books for many years.

 It is the only RV consumer organization in the world.

RV Consumer Group

publishes

The RV Rating Book

The RV Rating Book assists you in your search for the right RV. It is a complete reference book rating motor homes, travel trailer coaches, fifth wheel travel trailers, and tent trailers.

With thousands of models sorted by brand, type, and length, you will be able to compare RVs simply by looking at the ratings.

This book also gives you an analysis of each model's primary specifications.

The RV Rating Book

gives every model a

Highway Safety Rating

The highway safety rating represents the average handling characteristics of an RV when traveling on the highway and its ability to respond to driver commands. Weight, size, payload, and wheelbase-to-length ratio are primary safety factors for motor homes. Weight, size, payload, axle capacity, and hitch weight percentages are primary safety factors for travel trailers.

From our research into accident reports, the majority of accidents occur with RVs rated below 60 in *The RV Rating Book.*

The RV Rating Book

gives every model a

Durability Rating

Sixty percent of this rating is based upon the appraisal of thousands of used RVs from 5 to 10 years old. Our appraisers use a 50-point checklist to find out if a specific brand is showing signs of premature failure.

Twenty percent of this rating is based upon evaluations of new RVs. These evaluations determine how RV manufacturers are adhering to quality control of workmanship, materials, and design.

The remaining twenty percent is based upon RV owner satisfaction polls.

The RV Rating Book

gives every model a

Value Rating

 The value rating is important because it tells you about the depreciation rate and the investment factor. You don't want to buy an RV that depreciates to almost nothing in 5 years. You don't want to buy one that depreciates even to 60% of the original cost in 5 years.

The purpose of the value rating is to help you protect your investment.

The RV Rating Book

gives basic specifications, a price guide, and a livability code.

 By comparing specifications you'll soon get a good picture why some RVs are not safe to drive on the highway.

By studying the price guide you'll have a good idea of how much you'll be spending on any particular RV.

The livability code is important to everyone buying an RV. You'll want to know if any particular brand is designed for vacationing, RV trekking, snowbirding, or fulltiming use.

The RV Rating Book

gives

Star ☆ Awards

Star awards are given to those models that excel in highway safety, durability, and value. It's a model-by-model battle to get:

one ☆

two ☆☆ **or**

three ☆☆☆

Our star awards will help you make quick comparisons. Star awards are not easy to come by. Any model of any brand must satisfy our appraisers and the RV consumer to earn even one star.

Call RV Consumer Group and ask about —

The RV Rating Book

1996-1997 Edition $48

This book is designed to help you make selections in motor homes and travel trailers. Rates by highway safety, durability and value.

The Language of RVing

1997 Third Edition $28

A comprehensive guide of words and terms relating to buying and using RVs. Candid discussion with liberal use of photographs and drawings.

DealData Helpline

A low cost per minute question and answer session with an advisor for information relating to ratings, prices, discounts, and commentaries from our database about overall brand and model performance.

$18.50 up to 15 minutes — toll free number.

For current prices or to order call:

1-800-405-3325

May smart
RV consumers
and good
RV salespeople
meet in campgrounds
across America.

JD Gallant